I Saw a Bullfrog

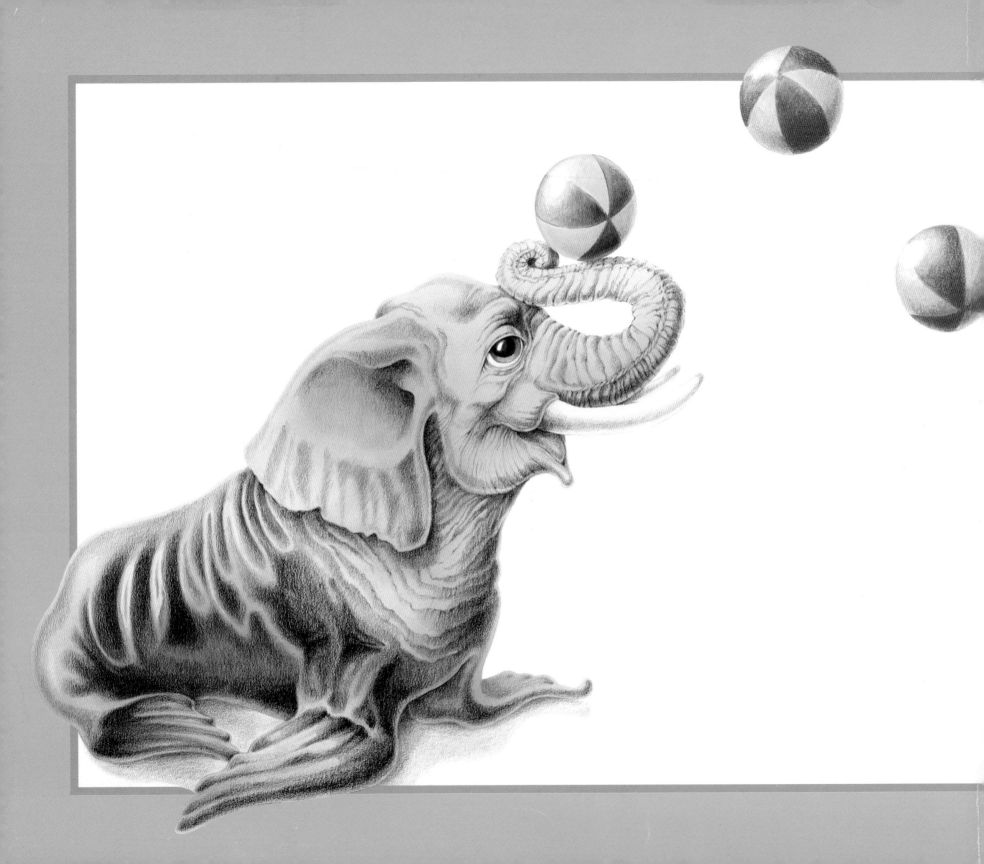

I Saw a Bullfrog

by Ellen Stern

Random House New York

About the Illustrations

The colored artwork for this book was executed on Crescent cold-press illustration board.
Liquitex acrylic paints were used to airbrush some areas and as color washes.
The painted surfaces were then worked over with Prismacolor pencils to create gradations and details.
The black-and-white illustrations were created on coquille board with a 6B pencil.

Published in the United States by Random House Children's Books, a division of Random House, Inc., New York,
and simultaneously in Canada by Random House of Canada Limited, Toronto.
www.randomhouse.com/kids

Library of Congress Cataloging-in-Publication Data
Stern, Ellen, 1944–
I saw a bullfrog / by Ellen Stern. — 1st ed.   p.   cm.
Summary: Rhyming text and illustrations reveal eleven animals with compound names,
such as a catfish, an elephant seal, and a dragonfly, as they would look if they were half one creature and half another.
Includes pictures of how each animal actually looks and facts about their unusual names.
ISBN 0-375-82173-2 (trade) — ISBN 0-375-92173-7 (lib. bdg.)
[1. Animals—Fiction. 2. Stories in rhyme.]   I. Title.
PZ8.3.S8287 Iae 2003   [E]—dc21   2002003659

Printed in the United States of America   First Edition   10 9 8 7 6 5 4 3 2 1
RANDOM HOUSE and colophon are registered trademarks of Random House, Inc.

For Ryan, with love

The bullfrog's a creature of which we've all heard,
But have you once paused to consider the word?
Is this an example of twisted linguistics
Or frogs that exhibit bull characteristics?

The following drawings are merely illusion,
But in the event they create some confusion,
When you get to the end, illustrated for you
Are the actual beasts. (It's the *least* I could do.)

I saw a **bullfrog** perched on a lily.

He was bigger than it, so he looked sort of *silly*.

Like a bull, he was sporting a ring in his nose,

But his front end had **hooves** while his back end had *toes*.

At the circus, I'll go see the **ELEPHANT SEAL**.

Should I take along peanuts or fish for his meal?

Do you think he'll have *flippers* or will he have toes?

Will he balance his ball on a **trunk** or a *nose*?

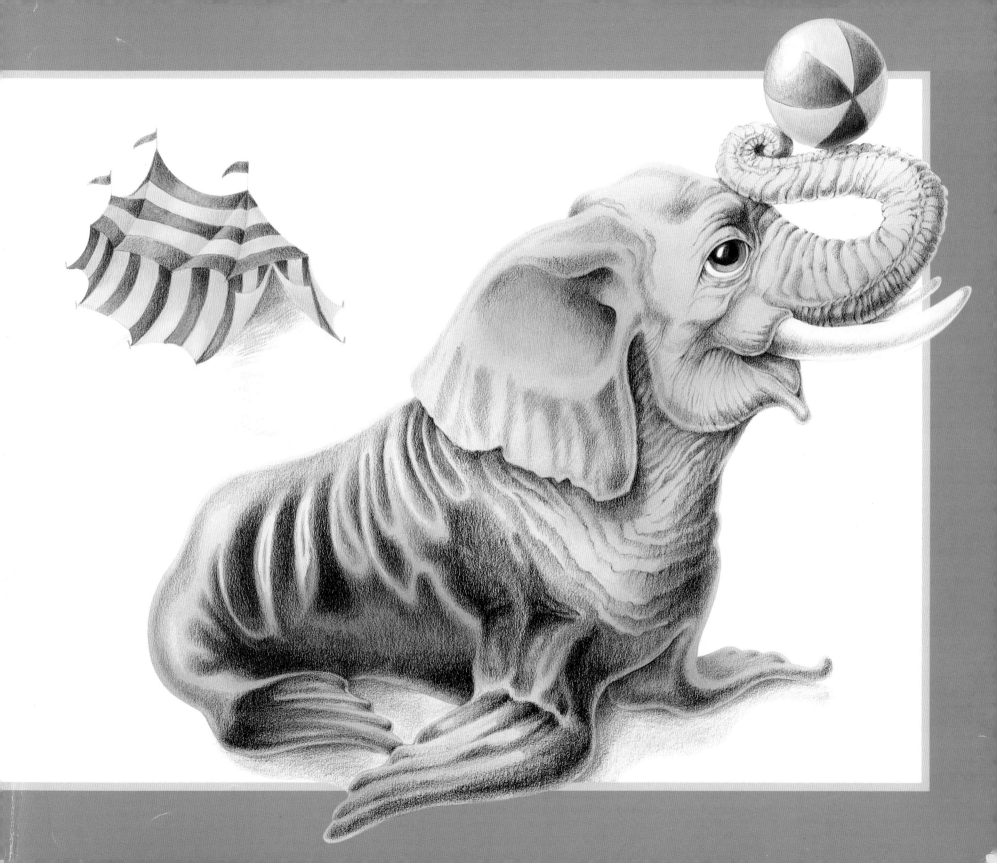

If a *catfish* could choose, would she snooze on my bed

Or swim round and round in a fishbowl instead?

Would she feel fishy-squishy or have fur soft as silk?

Would she turn up her nose at a bowl full of milk?

The **rhinoceros beetle** has a horn on his nose,

But how many *legs* has he? How many **toes**?

Is he **big** as a rhino or buggishly small?

Could he live in my bug jar or not fit at all?

If a RAT SNAKE is named 'cause you are what you eat,

Then he isn't a critter a rat wants to meet.

But if he's more rodent-like, bright-eyed and furry,

Then other small creatures have no need to worry.

The deer mouse turns out to be terribly shy.

Will she squeak with alarm if she sees you walk by?

For lunch, might she think that some seeds would be yummy?

Or does she prefer leafy greens in her tummy?

The tiger shark's name sounds so scary to me,

It isn't a creature that I'd like to see.

Would it pounce from a bush with a terrible ROAR?

Or prowl in the ocean far out from the shore?

If you saw a dragonfly all green and shiny,

Do you think he'd be **huge** or would he be *tiny*?

Would he live in a cave that's all SCARY and **dark**?

Or flit through the reeds in the pond at the park?

You'll find **goose barnacles** down at the ocean.

They don't have webbed feet or their own *locomotion*.

You won't hear them HONK; they don't **cackle** or **call**.

They just have a L o n g, goosey neck—and that's all.

I saw a **cowbird**, but she didn't moo.

Look up in that tree there and you'll see her, too.

This critter has *feathers* and never eats **HAY**.

If you tried to milk her, she'd just *fly away.*

Do you think that a **ZEBRA FISH** lives in a pool?

Might it *run* in a herd? Does it *swim* in a school?

Does it have fishy scales from its tail to its head?

Or look like a horse in **STRIPED PJ'S** instead?

BULLFROG

You wouldn't have to be very close to its pond to hear a bullfrog. The male's "jug o' rum" song can be heard as far as half a mile away. The bullfrog is the largest frog in North America. It eats bugs, other frogs, small fish, snakes, and even birds.

ELEPHANT SEAL

The elephant seal gets its name from its unusual nose, which can grow up to fifteen inches long. When the male gets angry, he blows his nose up like a balloon. Like an elephant, the male elephant seal is also very large and may weigh as much as eight thousand pounds.

CATFISH

The whisker-like feelers that give catfish their name are called barbels. All catfish have them. There are many different kinds of catfish in the world. The smallest is only an inch long, while another grows to ten feet. A variety of catfish that lives in Africa likes to swim upside down, and there's one in Florida that can walk on land. Some are dangerous: for example, the electric catfish can give a strong shock.

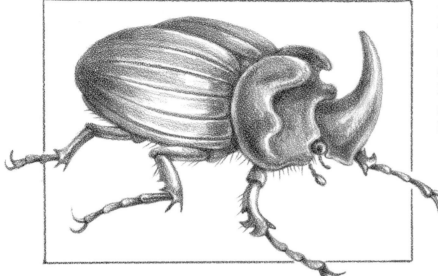

RHINOCEROS BEETLE

This is one of many beetles named after another animal because of the way they look or act. There are also tiger, tortoise, and stag beetles. The rhinoceros beetle gets its name from the large horn at the front of its head. There are other beetles that are named for what they eat, such as the potato beetle, asparagus beetle, bean beetle, and spotted cucumber beetle.

RAT SNAKE

The rat snake is named after one of its favorite snacks. These snakes also eat mice, lizards, and frogs. Sometimes they climb trees looking for small birds. They are very pretty snakes and come in a wide variety of colors. Rat snakes are easy to keep as pets, but watch out—they can grow to be as much as eight feet long!

DEER MOUSE

The coloring of the deer mouse is like that of a deer. These pretty little animals have brown or gray fur, with white bellies and feet. They live in hollow logs or in underground burrows, where they build rather messy nests of leaves, grass, and any other soft material they can find. Deer mice aren't very good housekeepers. When the old nest gets dirty, they just move out and build a new one.

TIGER SHARK

Besides the fact that they have stripes, tiger sharks are like tigers in other ways, too. Both are large animals with strong jaws and sharp teeth, and both can be dangerous to humans. Tiger sharks are often called "garbage cans with fins," since it seems they will eat just about anything. They have been known to snack on such tasty items as license plates, shoes, bottles, tiles, and tin cans.

DRAGONFLY

If you were a mosquito, it would be very scary to look up and see a large red, green, or blue dragonfly watching you with its enormous round eyes. You probably couldn't fly fast enough to get away because dragonflies can travel at up to sixty miles an hour. When flying, they use their six spiny legs to make a basket in which they trap their prey.

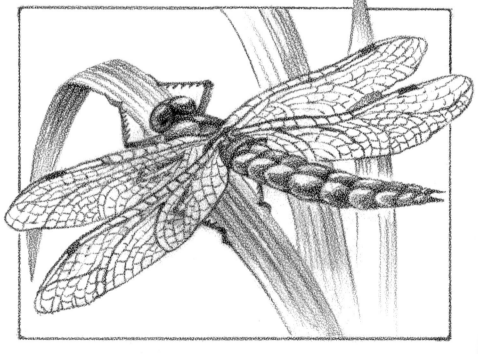

GOOSE BARNACLE

A goose barnacle has a long, goose-like neck, but it has neither feathers nor beak nor webbed feet. In fact, it doesn't have feet at all. Free-floating when young, the barnacle attaches itself to just about anything it bumps into in the ocean. Once it finds a home on a rock, a pier, a floating log, or even a passing whale, the barnacle stays there for the rest of its life.

COWBIRD

The cowbird gets its name from the fact that it will often follow a herd of cattle, gobbling insects that the cows' hooves churn up. The bird then returns the favor by removing ticks and other pesky hitchhikers from the cattle. The cowbird has plenty of time for these activities because it never bothers to build a nest. Instead, this bird lays its eggs in the nests of smaller birds, which must then spend much of their time feeding the large, greedy "adopted" babies.

ZEBRA FISH

If you have an aquarium, it's quite possible that you have some zebra fish. They are very easy to keep. You can see from their stripes why they are called zebras, but their stripes are dark blue and either gold or silver—not black and white like those of a four-footed zebra.

About the Author-Illustrator

Ever since she was a child collecting frogs, turtles, and the occasional snake,
Ellen Stern has been interested in wildlife.
A squirrel and a young robin were among her first companions.
She has worked in both fine arts and illustration in a wide variety of media.
A studio art teacher at Glendale Community College, she lives in
Los Angeles with her husband, her son, and a squirrel named Hoover—
after the vacuum cleaner.

E   Stern, Ellen
S   I saw a bullfrog

B

DATE DUE

JAN 11	DEC 0 2 '03		
Jul 24			
JUL 10 '03			
JUL 29 '03			
AUG 14 '03			
AUG 22 '03			
SEP 09 '03			
SEP 24 '03			
OCT 07 '03			
OCT 22 '03			
NOV 10 '03			
NOV 21 '03			

May 2003 *

Date_____

SEDRO-WOOLLEY PUBLIC LIBRARY
Sedro-Woolley, WA 98284